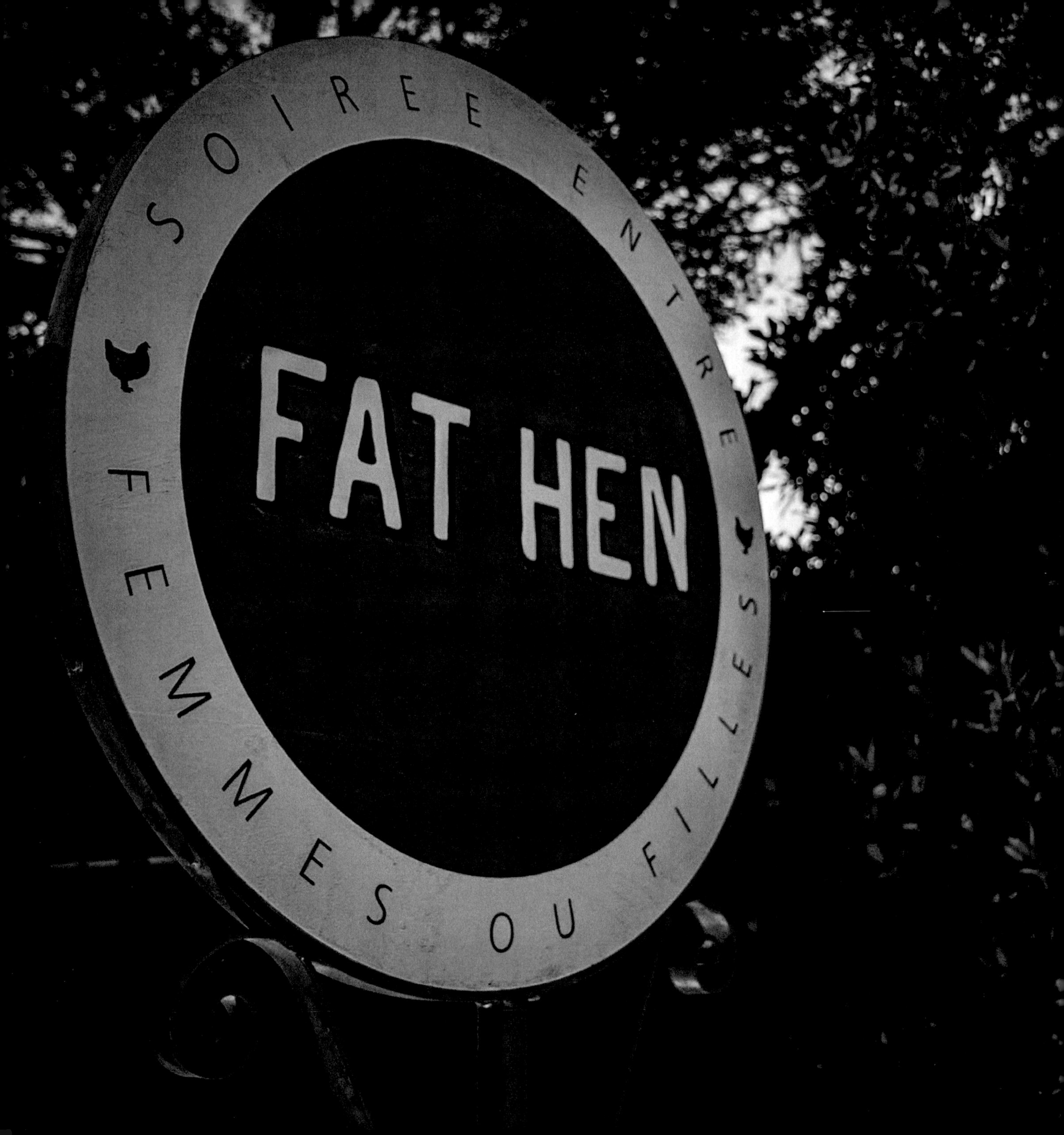
SOIREE ENTRE FEMMES OU FILLES
FAT HEN

Delicious Recipes Celebrating French Lowcountry Cuisine

The Fat Hen Cookbook

SOIRÉE ENTRE
FEMMES OU FILLES
FAT HEN

From The Kitchen Of Chef Fred Neuville

First Printing, 2015

ISBN 978-1512375626

Fat Hen
3140 Maybank Highway
Johns Island, SC 29455

www.thefathen.com

Food photography by Clayton Hyams.
Additional photography by Robert Smith.
Design and layout by Eve Eckman.

Thanks to the entire kitchen staff of Fat Hen.

Welcome to Fat Hen, a celebration of French Lowcountry cuisine and Charleston's rich Huguenot culture. The Huguenots were French Protestants influenced by the teachings of Martin Luther who established the French Reform Church in the 16th century and fled France to avoid persecution. In the late 1600s ships carrying dozens of families arrived in Charleston creating a Huguenot community that would attract hundreds of French Protestants over the next several decades.

The Huguenots who fled France were educated and skilled artisans, merchants, craftsmen, bakers and chefs coming from all areas of France - from the busy streets of Paris to the rustic French countryside. Along with their skills and religion, the Huguenots also brought with them their love of food and the combination of French cuisine and local ingredients became French Lowcountry cuisine. French cuisine is characterized by its devotion to fresh ingredients, expert preparation, and complete flavor combinations. Coupled with the bountiful produce, meats, and seafood of the area, French Lowcountry cuisine creates a regional character of cooking found nowhere else in America.

Fat Hen is committed to honoring the culinary history of French Lowcountry food through the creation of classic French preparations with the freshest local ingredients and by creating new classics in the spirit of the Huguenots. Examples of French Lowcountry include Duck Confit with Collard Greens and Squash, Flounder Nicoise over Bacon Cheese Grits, and Seared Grouper over Succotash.

Fat Hen offers innovative Lowcountry French cuisine using the freshest ingredients provided by their friends and neighbors in the farming community. Owned and operated by nationally acclaimed Chef Fred Neuville and his wife Joan, Fat Hen is located in the heart of the Johns Island farming community, minutes from downtown Charleston, South Carolina. Accompanied by a grand variety of local, regional, and international wines and beverages, Fat Hen serves dinner and Sunday brunch in a casual and comfortable atmosphere.

Chef Fred Neuville has been the founding chef and partner of some of Charleston's favorite restaurants. In 2007 Chef Neuville left to go out on his own with his family and open Fat Hen Restaurant (Lowcountry French). Neuville spent his days in the restaurant fast lane making an indelible mark on the Charleston food scene. Ready to fuse his passion for food and family, Neuville opened Fat Hen as an outpost for culinary delights and domestic enjoyment.

Table of Contents

Appetizers

Aioli Mussels
2 Portions

For the Garlic Butter

1 lb softened sweet unsalted butter
1 oz white wine
1 oz fresh lemon juice
1 tbls fresh chopped parsley
4 tbls minced garlic

Method

1) Mix all ingredients together and refrigerate.

For the Aioli - 1 Quart

1 cup whole peeled garlic
3 cups olive oil
3 egg yolks
2 tsp lemon juice
2 tbls kosher salt
4 oz water

Method

1) Roast the garlic in 3 cups of olive oil until tender and golden brown (Approximately 30 minutes at 350 degrees). When done, refrigerate until ready to use.
2) Strain the garlic and reserve the oil.
3) Puree the garlic and egg yolks together in a robo coupe or blender. Add lemon.
4) Slowly add the reserved garlic oil and water, alternating them.
5) Season with salt, adjust, and refrigerate until ready to use.

For the Mussels

1 lb Prince Edward Island Mussels cleaned and bearded
1/2 cup white wine
2-3 oz of garlic butter
1 tsp olive oil
Salt to taste

Method:

1) Heat a large sauté pan with the oil.
2) When the oil is almost at the smoking point, add mussels. When they begin to pop open, add white wine.
3) Gently toss your mussels, then when they are almost open all the way, add garlic butter and salt.
4) Stir in the butter with tongs.
5) Taste, adjust, top with the aioli using a squirt bottle and serve.

Beef Tartare
2 Portions

Ingredients

6 oz minced Butchers Steak (New York strip steak can be substituted)
16 capers
2 pinches of fresh picked herbs (parsley, chives, chervil, and tarragon)
4 tsp dressing
Salt and pepper to taste

For the Dressing

Yields 1 1/4 cups
1/4 oz anchovy fillet
3 1/2 oz Dijon mustard
5 oz fresh lemon juice
1 quail egg

Method

1) Make a paste out of anchovy fillets.
2) In a mixing bowl, add mustard, drizzle the lemon, add the anchovy paste.
3) Mix together with 4 tsp of dressing to make Tartare. Season beef with salt and pepper to taste. Serve with toast points, and quail egg.

Crab Cakes
8 4oz crab cakes

For the mix that binds the crab together

Yields 4 cups
1 qt mayonnaise
2 egg yolks
1/4 cup fresh lemon juice
1 tbls Old Bay seasoning
1/4 tbls kosher salt

Method

1) Mix all ingredients together.
2) Taste, adjust seasoning, and set aside in the refrigerator until ready to use.

For the Crab Cakes

1 lb lump crab
1/2 lb crab claw meat
3/4 cup crab mix
Paprika

Method

1) Pick through the crab removing any shell.
2) Mix with the crab mix.
3) Form the rest into 4 oz balls and refrigerate until ready to use.
4) When ready to serve, dust with paprika and place in a 350 degree pre-heated oven and bake until golden brown, approximately 10 minutes.
5) Serve with cocktail sauce, tartar sauce, and blue cheese bacon slaw (recipe on page 54).

9

Grilled BBQ Scallops with Pomegranate BBQ Sauce and Herb Salad
2 Portions

Ingredients

8 large sea scallops (10-20ct)
4 1/2 slices of apple wood smoked bacon (pounded thin)
4 oz picked herbs (tarragon, chives, parsley, and chervil)
1/4 oz blue cheese dressing (recipe on pg 29)
Salt and pepper to taste.

Method

1) Heat the grill.
2) Wrap scallops with thinly pounded bacon and skewer, season with salt and pepper
3) Rub a little olive oil on the scallops so they do not stick to the grill. Place on the grill, mark on all sides making sure the bacon is cooked.
4) When 3/4 of the way cooked baste the scallops with BBQ sauce (recipe on pg 79).
5) When they are done let them rest for 10 seconds. While they are resting toss the fresh herbs in blue cheese dressing (recipe on page 29) and place in the center of two plates. Remove scallops from
skewers and place around the herb salad. Enjoy!

Pimento Cheese
4 Portions

Ingredients
    1 cup cheddar cheese (shredded)
    3/4 lb cream cheese
    2 oz goat cheese
    1 cup roasted red peppers (minced)
    1 oz roasted and peeled jalapeño (minced)
    2 tsp kosher salt
    1/2 oz mayonnaise
    1/2 oz lemon juice
    1/4 tsp pepper

Method
1) Mince red peppers (food processor is best).
2) Mix with all other ingredients until smooth.
3) Taste, adjust seasoning, and serve.

Sautéed Oysters
1 Portion

Ingredients

1 oz shallots
1 1/2 oz country ham
1 1/2 oz wild mushrooms
1 oz white wine
3 oz liason (recipe on page 78)
1 oz spinach
5 oyster (selects)
1 tsp olive oil

Method

1) Using a sauté pan on high heat, render the ham in olive oil.

2) Add shallots and mushrooms. When the mushrooms are tender, add white wine.

3) Let the wine reduce by half and add liason (recipe on page 79).

4) When the liason is "nape" consistency (coats a spoon), add the spinach and oysters.

5) Poach the oysters until they begin to curl on edges, season with pepper, and serve over grilled fresh bread.

Soups

Crab Soup
1 Gallon

Ingredients

8 oz whole unsalted butter
2 cups flour
1 rib of celery (diced small)
1 medium size carrot (peeled and diced small)
1 medium yellow onion (peeled and diced small)
1/2 oz honey
1/2 oz worchestershire sauce
1/2 oz hot sauce
2 oz crab base (msg free)
3 oz dry sherry
2 quarts water
2 quarts heavy whipping cream
Salt and white pepper to taste
1/2 lb crab roe
Crab claw meat for garnish (1 oz per serving)

Method

1) In a large pot, sweat vegetables in the butter.
2) Add flour and stir constantly until it resembles wet sand and smells nutty (approximately 5 minutes).
3) Add honey, worchestershire sauce, crab base, and crab roe.
4) Add sherry and cook off the alcohol.
5) Whisk water and cream in slowly making sure to allow the liquid to be absorbed into the roux before adding more. This will insure smooth consistency
6) Bring to a boil and reduce to a simmer for 1 1/2 hours.
7) Puree the soup in a food processor and strain through a fine chinois.
8) Salt and pepper to taste.
9) Taste and adjust seasoning. Cool down in an ice bath and refrigerate until ready to serve.
10) When ready to serve, place desired amount of crab soup in a pot and heat up. Place 1 oz of crab in each cup. Pour hot soup over the crab and garnish with a teaspoon of crème fraiche (recipe on page 76) and a drizzle of dry sherry.

French Onion Soup
1 Gallon

Ingredients

    5 medium yellow onions (julienned)
    1/2 gallon chicken stock
    3/4 gallon veal stock
    3/4 cup sherry
    3/4 cup brandy
    1 1/4 oz kosher salt
    1/4 tsp fresh ground pepper
    1 tbls olive oil
    Sliced gruyere cheese
    Buttered toast points

Method

1) In a hot rondeau (or stock pot) add olive oil and bring to smoking point.
2) Add onions to hot rondeau to caramelize. Do not stir for two minutes, and after that, only stir every two minutes. (The reason you do not stir is that the onions will cook and release water and not caramelize.)
3) When onions are caramelized add both stocks and bring to a boil. Add the sherry and brandy and bring to a boil. Reduce to a simmer and cook until you have 1 gallon.
4) Season with salt and pepper and cool down. When ready to use, place on medium heat and bring back to a boil. Skim fat off of top. Adjust seasonings to taste.
5) Ladle into bowls. Place round toasts (buttered bread toasted and cut to desired size) in the soup and top with thinly sliced gruyere. Melt under the broiler at close range until the cheese is golden brown.

Truffle Potato Soup
5 Quarts

Ingredients
6 lbs peeled and quartered potatoes
chicken stock 3 qts or to cover potatoes
2 cups of heavy cream
1 oz white truffle oil
Salt and white pepper to taste

Method
1) Cook potatoes in chicken stock until done.
2) Purée until smooth.
3) Add heavy cream and truffle oil.
4) Heat and check consistency. Taste and adjust salt and white pepper.
5) Serve in a bowl garnished with fresh chives and crème fraiche.

Salads

Mesclun Salad
2 Portions

Ingredients

2 qt mesclun mix
1/2 peeled and julienne carrots
1/2 julienne zucchini
1/2 julienne yellow squash
3 strawberries sliced
2 oz red wine vinaigrette
3 oz roasted pecan halves
Salt and pepper to taste
1 tsp extra virgin olive oil

Method

1) Roast your pecan halves in a 350 degree oven, seasoned with the extra virgin olive oil and a little salt, for 5 minutes. Set aside to cool.
2) Wash vegetables and julienne them.
3) Toss in a bowl with the mesclun.
4) Season with salt and pepper and red wine vinaigrette. (Recipe on page 30)
5) Serve on a chilled plate.

Salads

Roasted Tomato, Corn and Boiled Peanut Salad
5 Portions

For the Tomatoes: 2 and 1/2 each

1) Wash, core and cut tomatoes into 1/8s.
2) Make the marinade: yield 4 cups
   1/4 cup olive oil
   1 1/2 cup balsamic vinegar
   1/3 oz minced garlic
   1/4 oz minced shallots
   1 bunch basil (chopped)
   1/4 bunch parsley (chopped)
   1/4 bunch chives (chopped)
   1/4 bunch fresh thyme (chopped)
   Salt and pepper to taste
3) Mix all ingredients together.
4) Taste the marinade and adjust the seasoning.
5) Marinate the tomatoes overnight.
6) Remove tomatoes from the marinade (save for another day or strain and use as a dressing).
7) On a 1/2 sheet pan with a roasting rack, place the tomatoes skin side down on the roasting rack with the sheet pan underneath.
8) Place in a 200 degree pre-heated oven and roast until the tomatoes are a quarter of the size. Be careful not to burn. Cool and refrigerate.

For the Corn: 1 and 1/2 ears

1) Shuck the corn and rinse off the corn silk.
2) Rub with olive oil, salt, and pepper
3) Either grill until charred on all sides or use broiler on high or gas burner.
4) When corn has cooled, remove from the cob and set aside.

For the Peanuts: 1 lb green peanuts

1) Cover peanuts with water. Season with 3oz of salt and 1/2 lb of either bacon or ham hock.
2) Bring to a boil and cook until tender, between 3 and 5 hours.
3) Remove peanuts and shuck when cool.
4) Refrigerate after shucking.

To assemble the salad:

1) Mix the corn, peanuts and tomatoes.
2) Add enough Green Goddess (recipe on page 29) dressing to just bind the ingredients together (2 tsp), season with salt and pepper, taste and adjust.
3) Add 1 oz each of fresh parsley, tarragon, chive sticks, and chervil.
4) 1 1/4 cup of mesclun greens per serving tossed with 1 tsp of green goddess dressing.
5) Place the greens on the plate and the peanut mixture on top of the greens
6) Garnish with diced tomato.

Blue Cheese Dressing
1 Quart

Ingredients

1 qt mayonnaise
1/2 tbls red wine vinegar
1/2 tbls honey
2/3 cup butter milk
1/2 tbls bacon fat
2/3 lb blue cheese crumbles
Season with salt and pepper to taste

Method

1) Blend all ingredients together with a whisk except the blue cheese crumbles.
2) Gently fold in the blue cheese crumbles.

Green Goddess Dressing
3 Cups

Ingredients

1/2 cup chopped parsley
2 oz fresh lemon juice
1 oz tarragon vinegar
2 cups mayonnaise
3 cloves garlic minced
1 1/2 fillets anchovy mashed
1 oz chives minced
1 tsp kosher salt
1 cup sour cream
Black pepper to taste

Method

1. Wash and chop herbs and then add the rest of the ingredients.
2. Whisk until all are incorporated.
3. Taste, adjust, and refrigerate until ready to use.

Red Wine Vinaigrette
3 Cups

Ingredients
- 5 oz red wine vinegar
- 1/2 oz Dijon mustard
- 1/2 oz honey
- 15 oz olive oil
- Kosher salt and fresh ground pepper to taste

Method
1) In a mixing bowl, whisk together honey and mustard, then add a little red wine vinegar to help start the emulsion.
2) Alternate oil and vinegar to make the dressing. Season, taste, adjust, then serve.

This is an emulsion of honey and mustard, which will only last 24 hours. If it breaks, start with the first step and drizzle in the broken vinaigrette.

Thousand Island Dressing
2 Quarts

Ingredients:
- 1 qt mayonaise
- 1 qt chili sauce
- 1/4 cup heavy cream
- 1/2 cup pickle relish
- Lemon juice to taste

Method:
1) Mix all ingredients together
2) Taste and serve

Entrées

BBQ Brisket
5 to 7 lb piece of brisket

Ingredients for the dry rub

2 oz ancho chili powder
2 oz chipotle powder
1/2 oz Old Bay seasoning
1 tsp coriander
1 tsp cumin
1/2 tbls paprika
1 tsp allspice
1/4 box dark brown sugar
Kosher salt to taste
Ground black pepper to taste

Method

1) Mix all ingredients together, taste, and adjust seasoning.

Ingredients for Braising Liquid

1 qt apple cider vinegar
3/4 box dark brown sugar
2 oz hot sauce
Salt and pepper to taste
1/2 tbls red pepper flakes
1/2 onion chopped
2 stalks celery chopped
1 bunch parsley stems
1 tbls garlic chopped

Method

1) Mix all ingredients together, heat to dissolve the sugar, taste, and adjust seasoning.

Method

1) Rub the brisket with dry rub. Let sit for 30 minutes at room temp. Then in a hot skillet, put 1 tbls of olive oil and sear on both sides. Place in a deep hotel pan and set aside.
2) Pour hot braising liquid over the brisket and cover with plastic wrap and foil.
3) Place in a preheated 350 degree oven and cook for 3 hours. Check it. (When done, the meat should pull apart easily.)
4) Let cool in the braising liquid for 4 hours.
5) Remove from the liquid and shred. Refrigerate.
6) Reduce the braising liquid by 1/2, strain, and add 1 cup to the bbq sauce (recipe on page 79).

Serving Suggestion

1) Slice fresh baked bread 1/2 inch thick. Grill or toast and set aside.
2) Heat brisket up with 6 oz BBQ sauce (recipe on page 79) and place on bread.
3) Top with blue cheese cole slaw (recipe on page 54) and slice in half, serve with a salad tossed in green goddess salad dressing (recipe on page 29).

Braised Pork Cheek Gumbo
10 Portions

For the cheeks

20 pork cheeks
1 onion
2 stalks celery
1 red pepper and 1 green pepper
5 cloves garlic (mashed)
1/2 cup balsamic vinegar
1 qt chicken stock
4 tbls tomato paste
Salt and pepper to taste
4 tbls olive oil

Method

1) Heat olive oil until it reaches smoking point.
2) Season cheeks with salt and pepper and sear in the oil.
3) Remove cheeks and set in a roasting pan.
4) Add onions, celery, and garlic. Cook until tender.
5) Add tomato paste and cook for 1 minute, then add balsamic vinegar.
6) Add chicken stock and ham hock after 2 minutes.
7) Cook for 1 1/2 to 2 hours at 250 degrees.
8) Remove from oven and let cool over night.
9) Remove from sauce and strain sauce. Reheat in sauce when ready.

For the Rice

4 cups rice
8 cups water
2 medium onions (diced small)
4 tbls fresh thyme
1 tbls olive oil

Method

1) Sweat onion in olive oil. Add the rice and cook for 1 minute.
2) Add herbs and water. Cook until done.

For the Okra and Tomatoes

1 medium onion (diced)
1 carrot (diced)
1 celery stalk (diced)
2 bell peppers (diced)
2 lb okra (sliced)
5 32oz cans of tomatoes
1 tbls chopped garlic
1 tbls olive oil

Method

1) Sweat onion, carrot, peppers, and celery until tender.
2) Add okra and tomatoes, cook for 45 minutes season with salt and pepper and add garlic. Taste and adjust seasoning.

For the Gumbo

1) Heat pork cheeks in sauce.
2) Plate over the hot rice and top with the hot okra tomato mixture.
3) Garnish with chopped parsley.

Butternut Squash Rice
4 to 5 14oz Portions

Ingredients
- 1 cup rice (2 cups water)
- 1 cup French green lentils (4 cups water)
- 3 cups butternut squash
- 2 medium sized yellow onions (caramelized)
- 10 each marinated tomatoes, rough chopped, (recipe on page 78)

Method
1) Put rice in water and cook until tender. Fluff with a fork and place on a pan in refrigerator
2) Put lentils in water and cook until tender (about 20 minutes). Strain and reserve the liquid. Place lentils on a pan in refrigerator.
3) Peel, seed, and medium dice squash. Toss in olive oil and season with salt. Place in a 350 degree oven and roast until tender (about 30 to 45 minutes). Set aside.
4) Peel 2 medium onions and julienne. In a hot pan with olive oil, caramelize onions. Set aside.
5) When squash and onions are cooled to room temp, mix with rice, lentils, and tomatoes. Refrigerate until ready to heat and serve.
6) To heat, add some of your lentil stock in a pan then add mixture and heat. Season with salt and pepper to taste. Garnish with goat cheese and serve. You also may add 2 oz garlic butter if you want. The stock should keep the mixture moist when heating up, remember you don't want soup.

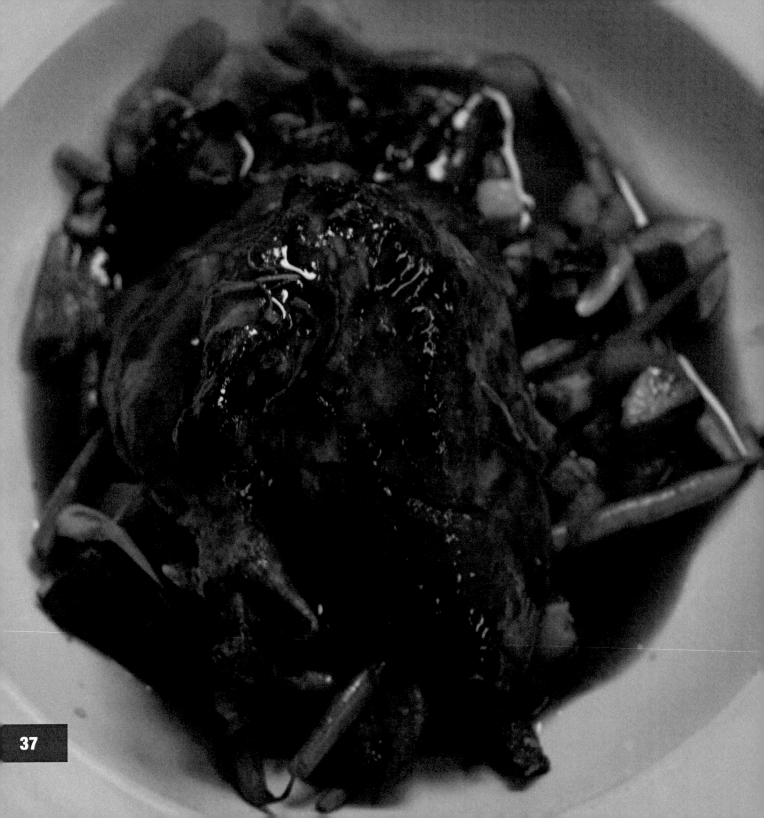

Coq au Vin
10 Portions

Brine for chicken: 1 3/4 gallons
1 1/2 yellow onions (chopped)
1 1/2 carrots (chopped)
1 1/2 ribs of celery (chopped)
12 1/2 bay leaves
1/4 cup chopped garlic
1/4 cup chopped shallots
1/4 cup chopped fresh thyme
1/2 tbls cinnamon
1/2 tbls allspice
5 cloves
2 cups sugar
1 1/4 cups Kosher salt
4 cups red wine
1 gallon hot water
3/4 gallons Ice

Method
1) Mix sugar, salt, and red wine. Add hot water and whisk to dissolve the sugar and salt.
2) Add rest of the dry ingredients, then add ice.
3) When ice has melted the brine is ready to use.

For the Chicken
5 chickens
2 yellow onions (medium and chopped)
3 carrots (rough chopped)
3 ribs of celery (rough chopped)
10 cloves fresh garlic
Sachet bag of 20 black peppercorns, 1/2 bunch fresh thyme, 1 bunch parsley stems, 4 bay leaves
1/2 gallon red wine (cooking wine)
2 gallons chicken stock or store bought broth
Salt and pepper to taste
1 cup tomato paste
48 oz canned diced tomato
3 oz olive oil

Method
1) Separate the chicken breast from the leg and thigh. You should have 4 pieces from each chicken.
2) Cover the chicken with brine for 2 days.
3) Pat the chicken dry. Season with salt and pepper.
4) In a rondeau (or stock pot), place olive oil and heat to the smoking point. Sear chicken quarters and place in a deep pan and set aside. The better the sear or color the better the flavor.
5) Add chopped vegetables (mirepoix) and whole garlic to the hot pan that you sautéed your chicken in and cook for 1 minute.
6) Add tomato paste, cook for 1 minute, stirring constantly. Add red wine and reduce by 1/2, then add canned tomatoes. Cook for 1 minute then add chicken stock. Bring to a boil, cover chicken with liquid.
7) Add sachet bag.
8) Cover pan with plastic wrap and aluminum foil. Put into a 250 degree pre-heated oven and cook for 1 1/2 hours. Uncover and check the chicken to make sure it is tender. The meat and skin should have pulled away from the leg end. Refrigerate in braising liquid for a least 4 hours.
9) After the chicken is cold. Remove chicken from liquid and debone rib bones of breasts. Wrap and refrigerate until ready to use.
10) On the stove, reduce sauce by 1/2 and refrigerate.
11) For the Garnish: 1/4 lb chopped bacon, 3 lb sliced button mushrooms, 1 lb blanched Haricot Verte. Render bacon. Add mushrooms and cook until tender. Add haricot verte and 10 oz of sauce and set aside.
12) Heat sauce and pour over chicken, place in a 350 degree oven uncovered until hot (10-15 minutes).
13) Place hot garnish in bowls, then the chicken.
14) Place sauce on stove and finish with 2 oz butter. Pour over top and serve.

Duck Confit
4 Portions

Ingredients

- 4 1/2 lb duck leg and thigh (8 each)
- 2 oz kosher salt
- 1 bay leaf
- 1 tbls fresh thyme
- 2 cloves garlic
- 1 tbls cracked black pepper
- 4 lb duck fat

Method

1) Mix all ingredients except duck fat and coat the raw duck.

2) Marinate for 24 hours.

3) Melt duck fat and add the marinated duck. Cover with plastic wrap and foil and cook at 250 degrees for 2 and 1/2 hours or until the leg meat pulls away from the bone.

4) Remove from oven, uncover, and place in the refrigerator.

5) Cool overnight. When ready to use, heat slightly to soften the fat and release the duck. Sear in a hot pan with olive oil skin side down for a nice brown color, flip and put in 350 degree oven until hot (approximately 10-15 minutes).

Flounder Nicoise
4 Portions

Ingredients
4 pieces 7-8 oz fresh flounder skin off
6 oz brown butter (recipe on page 75)
4 oz picked herbs (tarragon, chives, parsley, and chervil)
2 oz fresh squeezed lemon juice
2 oz capers
2 oz chopped Nicoise olives
6 oz fresh diced tomatoes
20 oz bacon cheese grits (recipe on page 52)
Salt and pepper to taste

Method
1) Season fish with salt and pepper. Put brown butter in a hot sauté pan and sear fish. Flip and cook for 1 to 2 minutes depending on the thickness of fillet.
2) Remove fish from pan and let rest keeping it warm.
3) Add capers, diced olives, and tomatoes. Cook for 10 seconds. Add lemon and herbs to the pan you cooked the flounder in.
4) Put hot grits in a serving dish, place fish on top and top with tomato-caper mixture.

Seared Grouper over Succotash
2 Portions

Ingredients

2 7oz pieces of fresh grouper (Use scamp, gag, or black. Do not use red because the texture can be rubbery at times)

4 oz wild mushrooms (seared)

4 oz Swiss chard (blanched)

2 oz corn (off the cob)

2 oz apple wood smoked bacon lardons (cooked)

2 oz leeks (julienne)

2 oz tomato (diced)

8 oz butter beans (cooked) (recipe on page 56)

2 oz garlic butter (recipe on page 80)

2 oz white wine

3 oz chicken stock (recipe on page 77)

1 oz olive oil

1 oz buerre blanc (recipe on page 75)

Salt and pepper to taste

Method

1) Heat oil in a sauté pan to smoking point. Season Grouper with salt and place in the pan.

2) Sear grouper on one side until golden brown. Flip and place in a pre-heated oven at 425 degrees. Cook for 8 to 12 minutes depending on thickness. Remove from oven and place in another pan, allowing the fish to rest. Keep warm.

3) In the pan you sautéed your fish in, add the white wine and reduce by 1/2.

4) Add all the mushrooms, Swiss chard, corn, leeks, and tomtoes, along with 2 oz of butter bean jus. Do not add garlic butter yet.

5) When the mixture is hot, add the garlic butter, season with salt and pepper.

6) In large bowls, spoon butter bean mixture and place the fish on top. Then spoon 1 oz of beurre blanc sauce on top and serve.

Shrimp & Crab Hoppin' John
3 Portions

For the Hoppin' John

Beans

- 1 cup dried black eyed peas
- 1 ham hock
- 2 cups water

Method

1) Rinse beans.
2) Put beans in medium sauce pot and cover with water. Add ham hock.
3) Bring to a boil and cook until tender (to speed up cooking time, soak beans overnight).
4) When beans are tender, strain and cool. Reserve ham hock.
5) When cooled, pick meat off of the ham hock and add back to the beans.

Rice

- 1/2 cup long grain rice
- 1/2 medium yellow onion (diced)
- 4 strips apple wood smoked bacon (diced)
- 1 tablespoon sweet butter
- 1/4 cup green onion (minced)
- 1 tablespoons lemon juice
- 3 oz hot sauce
- Salt and pepper to taste

Method

1) Render the bacon and sweat the onion until tender. Add butter and melt.
2) Add rice and cook for 30 seconds.
3) Cover rice with water (about 1 inch).
4) Cook until all liquid is gone and rice is tender.
5) Spread rice mixture on a sheet tray and cool.

Final Steps

1) Mix rice, beans, and green onion together. Season with hot sauce, salt, pepper, and lemon juice.
Remember, the mixture is cold, so do not over season. When the dish is reheated, the flavors will awaken.

For the final preparation

- 1 tsp olive oil
- 2 oz white wine
- 3 oz chicken stock
- 1/2 oz julienne zucchini
- 1/2 oz julienne squash
- 1/2 oz julienne carrot
- 1 oz garlic butter
- 25 shrimp peeled and deveined, tail off
- 3 oz jumbo lump crab meat
- 3 oz pimento cheese
- 3 oz blanched spinach

Method

1) In a sauté pan, add olive oil and heat to smoking point.
2) Add shrimp, sauté on both sides just to color. Then remove from pan and set aside.
3) Deglaze pan with white wine. Add julienne vegetables, hoppin' john, and chicken stock.
4) Add shrimp back to the pan along with the crab meat. Add spinach and pimento cheese. Stir in until melted.
5) Finish with garlic butter and season with salt and pepper.
6) Check seasoning. Place on a serving platter and garnish with chopped parsley.

Shrimp and Grits
6 Portions

For the Grits

1/2 qt grits
2 qt water
5 oz bacon, cooked and crumbled
4 1/2 cup half and half
1 1/2 cup parmesan cheese
2 tbsp vegetable oil
Salt and pepper to taste

Method for the Grits

1) Add water and half and half to a large pot and bring to a boil on high heat.
2) After the pot has come to a boil, turn down to a simmer (medium heat) and add grits. Stir frequently until grits become soft with no lumps and start to thicken up, about 10-12 minutes.
3) Next, add the parmesan cheese and whisk until smooth.
4) Salt and pepper to taste

For the Tasso Gravy

1 1/4 lb Tasso ham (small dice)
6 tbsp minced garlic
5 shallots (small dice)
3 1/4 cup white wine
1 3/4 qt heavy cream
2 1/2 oz lemon juice
To thicken, 1/4 lb Buerre Manie (equal parts soft butter & flour mixed together smooth)

Method for the Gravy

1) In a large sauce pot, add Tasso Ham and brown for 5 minutes. Add shallots and garlic.
2) Cook for 5 minutes until golden brown

3) When shallots and tasso have browned, add wine and reduce by half.
4) After wine has reduced by half, add heavy cream and reduce by half, (approximately 10-15 minutes.)
5) Add the Buerre Manie (equal parts flour and butter) and whisk until sauce has thickened. The sauce should coat the back of a spoon.
6) Cook for another 15 minutes, constantly whisking until the flour dissolves into the gravy and the gravy is smooth.
7) Season with salt and pepper.
8) Cool and refrigerate until ready to use

For the Shrimp & Assembly

2 lb (26-30) shrimp, peeled and de-veined
1 large red bell pepper (julienned)
1 large yellow bell pepper (julienned)
1 large green bell pepper (julienned)
1 medium yellow onion (medium diced)

Method for the Shrimp

1) Heat oil in large sauté pan on high heat
2) When oil is hot add shrimp. Sear the shrimp on both sides, remove shrimp from the pan and set aside.
3) Add peppers and onions. Sauté for 2 minutes or until peppers and onions are soft and tender.
4) Add 1/4 cup of the Tasso gravy. Adjust the thickness with chicken stock, if needed.
5) Add shrimp back into the gravy to finish cooking
6) When all ingredients have come together, taste and adjust seasoning, pour over the grits, and serve.

Sides

47

Bacon Cheese Grits
1 Gallon

Ingredients
1/2 qt stone ground white grits
2 qt water
4 oz half and half
1/2 qt shredded parmesan cheese
1 oz lemon juice
4 slices of apple wood smoked bacon (cooked and chopped)
1/2 lb butter
Salt and pepper to taste

Method
1) Bring water, half and half, and butter to a boil.
2) Add grits and stir, bring back to a boil.
3) Reduce to a simmer, stirring constantly for 1 hour to 1 1/2 hours or until tender.
4) Add cooked chopped bacon, lemon, and cheese. Season with salt and pepper.
5) Taste and adjust seasoning.
6) Cool and refrigerate grits until ready to use.
7) To heat place 1 cup milk in a pot, add grits, and constantly whisk until hot.

Blue Cheese Bacon Slaw
20-30 Portions

For the Slaw Mix
Makes 1 quart

    1 quart mayonnaise
    1/2 tbls red wine vinegar
    1 oz honey
    2 oz apple wood smoked bacon medium diced and
cooked
    3/4 lb blue cheese crumbles
    Season to taste with salt and pepper

Method

1) Blend all ingredients except blue cheese with a whisk.
2) Fold in the blue cheese.

For the Slaw
    2 cups slaw mix
    5 lb shredded cabbage

Method

1) Mix by hand until slaw is coated.
2) Serve chilled.

Butter Beans
30-40 Portions

Ingredients

10 lb butter beans
1 lb country ham, diced
3 carrots, cut to brunoise (1/8 inch squares)
1 bunch of chives
Chicken stock to cover by 1 inch

Method

1. Cook beans and ham in stock until tender, but not overcooked.
2. Cool in an ice bath and add carrots and chives.

Collard Greens
10 Portions

Ingredients

2 1/2 lb collard greens cleaned and washed
1 ham hock
1/4 lb bacon
1/2 onion (julienned)
1 cup apple cider vinegar
8 dashes hot sauce
Salt and pepper to taste
3 qt water
3 oz sugar

Method

1) Bring water, meats, and seasonings to a boil in a large pot
2) Tear or cut greens to desired size
3) Reduce heat to medium
4) Add greens and simmer until tender (approx. 1 hour)
5) Cool and refrigerate until ready to use.

Cream Corn
5 Portions

Ingredients

5 cups of fresh white or yellow corn off the cob
20 oz liason (recipe on pg 78)
Salt and pepper to taste
1 tbls diced shallot

Method:

1) Remove the corn kernels from the cob.
2) Heat the liason in a medium sized sauté pan.
3) Add the corn and shallots.
4) Season and serve when the corn is hot.

Potato Au Gratin
Yields 10 pieces, each 3 in. by 3 in.

Ingredients

8 large Idaho potatoes (peeled)
3 cups gruyere cheese plus 1/4 cup (grated) for the top
1 qt heavy cream
1 tsp black pepper
3 tsp kosher salt

Method

1) Mix cheese, cream, salt and pepper together with a whisk.
2) Slice potatoes on a mandolin thinly so you can just see your hand through the potato.
3) Toss potatoes in with the cheese mix and mix well.
4) Oil a 1/2 size shallow hotel pan (12"x10"x3" deep) and press the potato mixture into the pan and top with reserved 1/4 cup of cheese.
5) Bake at 250 degrees for 1 1/2 hours or until you see fat from the cream around the edges. When a knife is inserted in the middle there should be no resistance. Remove from oven.
6) Let it cool and cut in 3 in by 3 in squares and place on a pan. When ready, reheat at 350 degrees for 10 minutes and serve.

Crabcake Benedict
4 Portions

For the Crabcakes
(Make crabcakes according to recipe on page 8)

For the Hollandaise Sauce (yields 3/4 cup)
3 egg yolks
1/2 oz dry white wine
2 dashes of hot sauce
2 oz melted sweet unsalted butter
1/2 oz fresh lemon juice
Salt to taste
4 slices toasted bread

Method
1) Melt butter and set aside. Bring a pot of water to a boil.
2) Crack and separate egg yolks from whites. Place yolks in a metal bowl.
3) Add wine, hot sauce, and lemon to the yolks.
4) Whisk yolk mixture over pot of boiling water until yolks form a ribbon to the count of five. Remove from the heat.
5) Drizzle in melted butter while whisking continuously.
6) When done, sauce should coat the back of a spoon, season with salt.
7) Taste, adjust seasoning, and keep in a warm place until ready to serve.

To serve:
Put 1/2 a crabcake on each toast slice. Top with a poached egg and Hollandaise sauce, sprinkle with paprika and chopped parsley.

Crème Brulee French Toast
10 Portions

For the Batter (Yields 1 Qt)

1/2 lb sugar
8 egg yolks
3 vanilla beans
2 cups heavy whipping cream
1 cup whole milk

Method

1) Split vanilla beans length wise and scrape the seeds out reserving the pods.
2) Whisk together egg yolks, sugar, vanilla seeds and pods. Slowly whisk in cream and milk.
3) Put mix in a plastic container, cover, and refrigerate for 24 hours.
4) Strain through a sieve, skim off the foam, and stir with a rubber spatula to evenly distribute the vanilla bean seeds

For the Toast:

30 pieces thick sliced bread

Method

1) Pre-heat skillet on medium heat. Add vegetable oil (just enough to coat). When the oil is hot, dip three slices of bread in the batter on both sides then place on your skillet.
2) Brown both sides, remove from skillet. Plate and serve, topped with syrup, fresh fruit, or strawberries marinated in orange liquor.

Pulled BBQ Duck Sandwich
8 Portions

For the Duck
32 oz pulled duck confit
(recipe on page 40)

For the BBQ Sauce
16 oz of pomegranate BBQ sauce
(recipe on page 79)

For the Slaw
8 oz blue cheese bacon slaw
(recipe on page 54)

Method
1) Remove duck meat from bone, discard skin.
2) Heat on low heat with sauce.
3) Serve 4 oz of duck on a bun topped with 1 oz of
slaw.

Quiche
3 Quiches

For the Dough (Yields 3 deep dish pie shells)

11 oz softened butter
2 oz cream cheese
1 oz sugar
1/4 oz salt
1/4 tsp garlic powder
3/4 lb cake flour
1/4 lb all purpose flour
1/2 tbls white vinegar
1/2 cup water (lukewarm)

Method

1) In a mixer, cream butter, salt, sugar, and cream cheese
2) Mix the rest of the dry ingredients together and slowly add to creamed butter mixture
3) Add wet ingredients
4) Mix for 3 minutes. The dough should come away from the sides of the bowl. Remove from the bowl and divide into 3 equal balls.
5) On a table with a small amount of flour, roll each ball to a 1/4 in. thickness and place in greased quiche pan, pressing down to fit. Cut any dough off that's more than an inch and set aside
6) Place a piece of parchment inside dough and fill with rice or dry beans. Place in a pre-heated 325 degree oven and bake for 20 to 30 minutes or until the edges are golden brown.
7) Let cool down and then remove the parchment and the beans. (Make sure none of the beans have gotten in the dough.) Check for cracks. If you have a crack take a little left over dough, moisten it and spread over your crack.

For the filling

10 large eggs
1 qt heavy whipping cream

For the topping mix

Shredded cheese such as cheddar or swiss
Crumbled bacon
Diced and seeded tomato
Blanched spinach (water squeezed out)

Method

1) Fill 1/2 way with shredded cheese
2) Add bacon, tomato, and spinach.
3) Whisk eggs and cream together and season with salt and pepper.
4) Pour over ingredients to the top of quiche pan.
5) Place on a sheet pan in a pre-heated 325 degree oven for 45 minutes to 1 hour or until the quiche are set. Use a toothpick to check the center if it comes out clean you are done.
6) Let cool. Then slice into 8 slices and serve. Reheat in the microwave for 2 minutes if needed.

With a quiche, the only limitation is your own imagination. In place of the spinach, tomatoes, and bacon almost any combinations of cheeses, meats, and vegetables can be used in the topping mix to make a delicious quiche.

Brown Butter

Ingredients
1/2 lb butter (2 sticks)

Method
1) Melt butter and brown while skimming the milk solids from the top.
2) Set aside until ready to use. It should be brown in color and nutty in taste.

Buerre Blanc
Yields 1-2 Cups

Ingredients
1/4 cup heavy cream
1 cup white wine
1/2 cup chicken stock
1 tsp shallots
1 tsp garlic
1/2 lb butter
Salt and pepper to taste

Method
1. Put wine, shallots, and garlic in sauce pot. Reduce by half.
2. Add chicken stock, bring to a boil, and reduce by half.
3. Add heavy cream and reduce by 1/4.
4. Whisk in butter. When butter is melted, season and strain, keeping sauce warm, but not hot.

Cheese Mixture for Grilled Cheese
Yields 3 lb

Ingredients

1 lb goat cheese
1 lb shredded swiss cheese
1/2 lb shredded parmesan
1 oz lemon juice
1/4 cup fresh basil chiffonade
1/4 cup sundried tomatoes (diced small)
1 tbls minced shallot
Salt and pepper to taste

Method

1) Blend all ingredients until smooth. Fold in basil.
2) Use in place of sliced cheese in grilled cheese sandwiches.

Crème Fraiche
Yields 5 oz

Ingredients

3 oz sour cream
1/2 oz heavy whipping cream
1/2 oz fresh lemon juice
1 oz buttermilk
Salt and pepper to taste

Method

1) Mix all ingredient together and season
2) Taste and adjust

Chicken Stock
Yields 1 Gallon

For Sachet de Garni
6 inch x 6 inch piece of cheese cloth or muslin
Butchers twine
3 bay leaves
6 sprigs of parsley

Method
1. Put all ingredients into sachet, bundle together at the top and tie firmly with the butchers twine.
2. Maybe used for stocks, soups, braising liquids, or anything that you want to add more flavor.

For the Stock
5 lbs of fresh chicken bones cleaned
1 gal of cold water
2 large carrots peeled and diced
2 medium onions diced
5 stalks celery diced
1 sachet de garni

Method
1. Place all trimmed bones into a large stock pot and cover with cold water (more or less can be added depending on the amount of bones). Add carrots, onion, and celery and bring to a boil.
2. Turn stock down to a simmer and skim as needed.
3. When reduced by a third, strain through a fine meshed sieve. If not using stock right away, refrigerate and store. Stock can be frozen or used within three days.

Liason

Ingredients

1 qt heavy cream
4 egg yolks

Method

1) Heat cream to a simmer and remove from fire
2) Separate yolks from the whites.
3) Whip yolks.
4) Add a little hot cream and whisk constantly to temper the yolks.
5) Add rest of cream while whisking and put pot back on stove. Heat just long enough to allow the yolks to thicken the cream.
6) Remove pot from the stove, strain, and refrigerate until ready to use.

Marinated Tomatoes
Yields 4 Cups

Ingredients

10 tomatoes
3 cups balsamic vinegar
1/2 cup oil
1/4 lb basil chiffonade
1/2 bunch fresh thyme
1/2 bunch fresh parsley
1/2 bunch chives
1/2 cup minced shallots
1 oz minced garlic
Salt and pepper to taste

Method

1) Mix all ingredients. Taste and pour over quartered tomatoes
2) Marinate overnight. Lay tomatoes seed side up in a 250 degree oven for about 1 1/2 hours to 2 hours to dry them out.
3) Cool and refrigerate until ready to use.

Pomegranate BBQ Sauce
Yields 1 Quart

Ingredients
1 lb dark brown sugar
6 oz pineapple juice
16 oz pomegranate juice
1/4 cup molasses
5 oz Picka Peppa sauce
1 1/4 cup tomato paste
1 tbls ground chipotle
1 tsp ground ancho chili
1 1/2 tbls Kosher salt

Method
1) Mix all ingredients together, taste, and adjust seasoning

Red Pepper Jelly
Yields 2 Cups

Ingredients
2 1/2 red peppers
1/2 jalapeno
1/2 cup Champagne vinegar
1/2 cup sugar
1/2 cup orange juice
1 tsp pectin

Method
1) Cut red peppers and jalapeno in half. Clean seeds and white pith, dice small.
2) Mix pectin and sugar together and set aside.
3) Combine red peppers, jalapeno, vinegar and orange juice in a small sauce pot.
4) Cook until peppers are tender.
5) Add pectin and sugar mixture by whisking it in.
6) Remove from stove and chill until ready to use.

Roquefort Grapes
Yields 37 Portions

Ingredients
37 red seedless grapes
1/2 cup cream cheese
1/2 cup blue cheese crumbles
2 cups roasted pecans (seasoned with olive oil and salt)
Salt and pepper to taste.

Method
1) Leave the cream cheese and blue cheese out at room temperature until soft. Mix together and set aside until ready to use.
2) Wash grapes and dry them.
3) Grind roasted pecans.
4) Roll grapes in cheese mixture then in ground pecans.
5) Refrigerate until ready to use.

Great for a passed hors d'oeurve

Shallot or Garlic Butter
Yields 1 lb

Ingredients
1 pound sweet unsalted butter
1 tbls fresh chopped parsley
1 1/2 oz minced shallot or garlic
1 tsp white wine (cooking wine)
1 1/2 tsp fresh squeezed lemon juice

Method
1) Let butter sit out until soft.
2) When butter is soft, mix all ingredients together and taste, adjust seasoning
3) Set aside what you are going to use and portion the rest in 1 oz pieces and freeze for later use. This is great over fish, chicken, beef or to finish a sauce.

This is a great base recipe you can change out the shallots for garlic or any number of other ingredients, such as sun-dried tomatoes or capers. You can also add other herbs to it like dill, chives, tarragon, or fennel.

Sweet Pepper Relish
Yields 3 Cups

Ingredients

1 1/2 yellow peppers
1 1/2 red peppers
1 1/2 green peppers
1/2 cup sugar
1/2 tsp salt
1 and 1/2 cups cider vinegar

Method

1) Cut peppers in half and remove the pith and seeds.
2) Dice peppers (small) and place in a medium sauce pot.
3) Put rest of ingredients in pot and cook until peppers are tender.
4) Remove and refrigerate until ready to use.

Tomato Jam
Yields 2 Cups

Ingredients

1 1/2 cup tomato paste
1/2 jalapeno (without seeds)
1/2 cup Champagne vinegar
1/4 cup sugar
2 cups canned diced tomatoes
1 tsp kosher salt

Method

1) Combine all ingredients and cook down until thickened to 2 cups.
2) Puree in a food processor, taste, and adjust seasoning.
3) Refrigerate until ready to use.

When fresh tomatoes are in season use them in place of canned.

29358856R00051

Made in the USA
Middletown, DE
16 February 2016